Pebble®

LET'S LOOK

LET'S LOOK AT
GREECE

Nikki Bruno Clapper

raintree

a Capstone company — publishers for children

Raintree is an imprint of Capstone Global Library Limited, a company incorporated in England and Wales having its registered office at 264 Banbury Road, Oxford, OX2 7DY – Registered company number: 6695582

www.raintree.co.uk
myorders@raintree.co.uk

Edited by Carrie Sheely
Designed by Juliette Peters
Picture research by Tracy Cummins
Production by Laura Manthe
Originated by Capstone Global Library Limited
Printed and bound in India

ISBN 978 1 4747 5307 4 (hardback)
22 21 20 19 18
10 9 8 7 6 5 4 3 2 1

ISBN 978 1 4747 5313 5 (paperback)
22 21 20 19 18
10 9 8 7 6 5 4 3 2 1

British Library Cataloguing in Publication Data
A full catalogue record for this book is available from the British Library.

Acknowledgements
We would like to thank the following for permission to reproduce photographs: Getty Images: Jamie Squire, 17; Shutterstock: Antoine2K, 21, dinosmichail, 8–9, Evgeni Fabisuk, 11, franco lucato, 14–15, fritz16, Cover Top, Globe Turner, 22 Top, irakite, 10, Irma eyewink, 12-13, Joshua Resnick, 18, Korpithas, 6–7, krivinis, Cover Bottom, Cover Back, Lev Paraskevopoulos, 5, Mila Atkovska, 22–23, 24, nale, 4, Pawel Kazmierczak, 1, 19, Romas_Photo, Cover Middle, VOJTa Herout, 3

Every effort has been made to contact copyright holders of material reproduced in this book. Any omissions will be rectified in subsequent printings if notice is given to the publisher.

All the internet addresses (URLs) given in this book were valid at the time of going to press. However, due to the dynamic nature of the internet, some addresses may have changed, or sites may have changed or ceased to exist since publication. While the author and publisher regret any inconvenience this may cause readers, no responsibility for any such changes can be accepted by either the author or the publisher.

CONTENTS

Where is Greece?

Greece is a country in southern Europe. It is about the size of England. Greece's capital is Athens.

Greece

Islands and mountains

Three seas circle

Greece's mainland.

More than 2,000 islands

dot the seas. Some beaches

have red or black sand.

Much of Greece's land is rocky. Mountains cover the mainland. Greece has active volcanoes.

In the wild

Wild goats climb

Greece's steep mountains.

Pelicans and other water

birds live on the coast.

Starfish cling to rocks.

wild goats

pelican

People

People have lived in Greece for 2,500 years. Many people came from other parts of Europe or from Asia.

At work

Many Greeks work
in tourism. Others grow
olives or catch fish
for a living. Some families
own small businesses.

olive picking

Olympic birthplace

Sports are important

in Greece. The Olympic

Games started there.

Football and basketball

are favourite Greek sports.

At the table

Greeks have a healthy diet.

They eat lots of seafood,

olives and vegetables.

They snack on grape leaves.

Baklava is a sweet treat.

baklava

A famous site

The Acropolis sits on a
hill in Athens. It has
many ancient temples.
Thousands of people
visit the Acropolis every day.

QUICK GREECE FACTS

Greek flag

Name: Hellenic Republic

Capital: Athens

Other major cities: Thessaloniki, Larisa, Patras

Population: 10,773,253 (July 2016 estimate)

Size: 131,9657 square kilometers (50,949 sq mi.)

Language: Greek

Money: euro

GLOSSARY

active currently erupting or likely to erupt

ancient from a long time ago

baklava sweet treat made of dough and filled with nuts

capital city in a country where the government is based

mainland main part of a country that also has islands

temple building used for worship

tourism business of taking care of visitors to a country or place

volcano opening in the earth's surface that sometimes sends out hot lava, steam and ash

FIND OUT MORE

BOOKS

Greece (Explore the Countries), Julie Murray (ABDO, 2015)

Cultural Traditions in Greece (Cultural Traditions in My World), Lynn Peppas (Crabtree, 2013)

Greece (Exploring World Cultures), Kate Shoup (Cavendish Square, 2017)

WEBSITES

http://www.bbc.co.uk/guides/z36j7ty
Find out how the Olympic Games began in Greece.

http://www.natgeokids.com/uk/discover/history/greece/10-facts-about-the-ancient-greeks/
Discover some fun facts about ancient Greece.

http://www.bbc.co.uk/schools/primaryhistory/ancient_greeks/athens/
Discover the history of ancient Greece.

COMPREHENSION QUESTIONS

1. How do you think the mountains and volcanoes might affect how people live and travel on Greece's mainland?

2. Look at the photo on page 11. What features do pelicans have that might help them live near water?

3. What is a capital?

INDEX